HELEN DAHLHAUSER

BEFORE

YOU

LEAVE

End with Love

ISBN 978-0-9797987-0-2

FIRST EDITION

Published by Helen Dahlhauser

Editor, Sandi Corbitt-Sears, *Three View Design*
Designer, Diane Papadakis (Pakaáge), *Three View Design*

Additional information for Helen Dahlhauser is available on line at
www.before-you-leave.com

Prologue

On the surface, *Before You Leave* might appear to be a manual for leaving a relationship, but it is anything but that. Let me share with you how the idea for this book came about.

I have a partner with whom I've worked for almost 20 years. He has always been quite invested in keeping couples together. I feel pretty detached about the outcome. Strangely, we have noticed that some of the most challenging couples working with me have healed while my partner has had a few breakups happen right in the office. One man strode to the restroom and flushed his wedding ring then and there.

It's not that my business partner isn't good at what he does. He is a very talented therapist who is perhaps better than I am at helping people to let go more quickly. Each of us has strengths and weaknesses, and I am coming from my perspective. My non-attachment to outcome gives me permission to ask certain questions and explore areas he sometimes avoids. I often ask couples about divorce and try to remove their fears about it. I challenge them to stay in the relationship not because they are afraid of being single, but because they love each other and want to be together. I point out that it is a much deeper commitment to stay when leaving holds no fear for you.

When people who are comfortable with the prospect of divorce and going it alone choose instead to stay in a relationship, it builds trust. Both partners know it's not because of the kids or fear of a future outside the marriage.

The paradox in my work is that the more I give permission to leave, the more likely people are to heal their relationships. I attempt to apply this paradox to my personal life, as well (wouldn't I be quite the hypocrite if I didn't?). My spiritual beliefs lend themselves to nonattachment. Yet, when I don't succeed, I get attached and want things to work out. Then I have to remind myself about my own formula for detachment. It works, even for people as imperfect as I am.

It creates a lonely feeling when you suspect that you're wanted only because you're financially successful, a nurturing supporter, or an attractive arm piece. But to be wanted because of who you are, complete with your quirks, failings, and unique needs, is the warmest feeling in the world. You might cry at cheesy movies and crave fresh flowers and real Christmas trees. You might be a pain in the neck with a need to express your feelings when your partner wants to forget it and go to sleep. But that's who you are, and you want to be loved for those qualities (or, at least, in spite of them). Sure, we like being considered beautiful and having someone special express pride in our accomplishments. But what we need is to be loved for who we are inside.

I don't want to mislead you into thinking that nonattachment to outcome will heal relationships automatically. Plenty of the couples who have worked with me separate in the end. But by going through the process I outline in this book, they are so much more complete and so much more prepared for the future that the guilt and regret they experience is minimal.

From personal experience, I can attest to the remarkable difference between ending a relationship in the "usual" way versus ending with love. Best of all, leaving with love can apply not only to marriage and other intimate relationships, but to friendships and close professional partnerships. Those of you with the courage to embrace the process described in the following sections will be rewarded with grace, inner healing, and great self-love. It is my hope that reading this will bring you a richer life and closer relationships.   *Sincerely* — Helen Dahlhauser

Introduction

I want to reach for you
Keep you forever young and golden
I glaze my eyes so I don't see
The efficient stranger
Kissing me meaninglessly
As he turns away

I remember a tall, gangly boy in San Francisco with straight brown hair falling over his forehead. On an exquisite, crisp, and sunny day his eyes crinkled with humor and love. He bent to kiss me as he pinned flowers on my coat. Then we explored the city hand in hand, planning our future together.

I remember the same boy as he stood awkwardly in the delivery room. His lower lip trembling, he said, "I guess her father can hold her." As he held his daughter in his arms for the first time, the look of love and tenderness on his face forever touched my heart.

In another flash of memory, we're playing in the snow. He is unshaven, laughing, wearing an old sweatshirt. I felt so safe and warm. I thought in that moment we would be together forever.

But the boy with the laughing eyes, the father with the tender smile, the man I'd tumbled with in the snow, slowly became a stranger in a business suit. We had once said, "I do," but I was beginning to think, "I don't," and it was heart wrenching.

My story is personal, but it echoes the experience of countless couples who are faced with the decision to continue or to end the relationship they have formed together. In more than twenty years of counseling men and women in relationships, I have seen people handle this difficult choice in many different ways. I have come to understand that we all go through several key steps in the process of ending (or continuing) a relationship. I share these steps with you in the hope that they will bring more awareness, clarity, and insight to your own journey.

As you begin to work through the steps, you may think, "I know I'm unhappy, but this process is going to take forever." I assure you it doesn't need to take more than a few months, and whether you ultimately stay or go, the end result will be so much better than it might otherwise have been. Any time you spend on these steps will be repaid many times over in terms of your future happiness, self-confidence, and relationship success. I can make that statement with confidence because it's what I have been told by the many clients I have guided on this journey. If you are ready to join them, let's begin. ~ Helen Dahlhauser

Table of Contents

―――

CHAPTER 1

AWARENESS of Dissatisfaction

*I close my eyes
and see the path in front of us
My heart opens
when I see the sharp turn that I take away from you.
Can't we recapture the magic?*

When a relationship follows the path you anticipated when you first fell in love, the connection grows deeper as time passes. Conflicts are resolved quickly through communication and mutual trust. You move together toward a future designed to fulfill your individual and combined needs.

But some relationships diverge from the hoped-for path. When that happens, you may feel an aching emptiness even when you're having fun. You look at your partner and barely recognize him. A gnawing sense of foreboding makes you dread going home each evening, and goodbye hangs in the air whenever you and your partner spend time together. Something significant has changed between you, but you can't quite identify what it is or why it's happening.

During this time you may consciously (or subconsciously) try to reignite the love you once shared by planning romantic weekends or revisiting familiar places. You do all the things that used to bring you closer, but you can't completely escape the fact that it just isn't working anymore.

Most relationships don't fall apart in the space of a day or a week. It's a gradual, often subtle process that builds over time. At some point, the signs of trouble become impossible to ignore or explain away and one or both partners become aware of their dissatisfaction with the relationship.

DENIAL

This awareness is handled either directly or indirectly, depending on the way each individual typically approaches conflict. Indirect approaches such as denial and avoidance, while unhealthy, are all too common. Many of us prefer to ignore problems in the hope that they will go away on their own, which is the essence of denial. Since awareness can be a lengthy process, it's easy to continue to pretend that nothing is wrong. Denial doesn't solve the problem, but it can allow you hide from the pain of an ailing relationship… for awhile, at least.

AVOIDANCE

Avoidance doesn't deny the existence of problems, but relies on diversions and distractions to protect you from having to face the truth. On some level, you know something is wrong, so you throw yourself into activities such as overwork, over involvement with your children, frequent illness, endless projects, excessive volunteer work, or affairs. Some of these forms of avoidance appear to be more respectable than others, but having an affair is really no different than obsessing on volunteer activities in terms of the energy, time, and attention spent away from the primary relationship. Anything that's done to excess can be a symptom of avoidance.

However, because they're so common (and so destructive), I feel compelled to make a special point about affairs. If you are tempted to have an affair as a way of dealing with (or avoiding) the problems in your relationship…don't. I say this not from a place of judgment, but from pure pragmatism. Affairs create much deeper wounds and make the dissolution of a relationship infinitely messier. If it doesn't work out with the third person, he/she may be confused by your motives when you eventually end that relationship, and you could be plagued with guilt for years to come. If your current union is so troubled that you must leave, end it cleanly so that your future direction will be clear.

FACE YOUR FEARS

While it's tempting to push away the truth through denial and avoidance, until you gain awareness that something's wrong, it cannot become right. The first step is admitting that your relationship has changed and then facing the fear that it will end. Unfortunately, many couples wait so long to find the courage to verbalize their dissatisfaction that it's too late to salvage the relationship. Waiting won't get you the boy with the laughing eyes or the man you wrestled with in the snow. It won't get you what you desire for your relationship.

If you continue to limp along in a state of dissatisfaction, you face the prospect of being left by your partner or living only half a life. A bad relationship may eventually curdle and then petrify, leaving both people with a generalized apathy toward life. Their relationship becomes merely an endurance contest that brings happiness to no one.

The faster you admit and voice your dissatisfaction, the greater the chance your relationship can heal.

Human beings do change. In fact, they need change. Whether the end result of healing your relationship is years of happiness together or ending the relationship in a loving way, facing the changes that have occurred is necessary. It's an ongoing process and not an easy one, but it's the only way to live vibrantly in your relationships.

EXAMPLE

Gaining awareness that your relationship has serious flaws is one of the most difficult steps in the process of building happy relationships. It was certainly hard for Joan, who was married to a very successful man. They had two young children and her husband provided for his family beautifully. But he was gone all the time.

Her aunt, who lived with them as a nanny, catered to Joan's husband and continually told her niece to be grateful for all she had. Joan was miserable, sensing something was wrong, but she didn't feel she had the right to talk about it. When her aunt went away for an extended period of time, Joan finally admitted how truly alone she felt and timidly came to me for counseling.

Joan gradually worked up the courage to look closely at her relationship and learned that her feelings counted, regardless of how much she had to be grateful for. Her frequent headaches miraculously disappeared once she became honest with herself and admitted that she was, indeed, unhappy.

As Joan learned to let herself feel what she felt without judging the emotions, she began to take greater responsibility for making herself happy. She joined a gym, took a college course, and played with the idea of buying a day care center. Her self esteem grew and she found the courage to question (not nag) her husband and to listen carefully to his answers. She had known things weren't adding up and that something was wrong. It turned out her husband was on the verge of a collapse due to excessive drinking while he was away from home.

Joan's growing sense of self worth helped her give him an ultimatum:

the drinking or his family. Fortunately, this story has a fairytale ending. After much pain and work on both sides, Joan's husband became sober, and the couple recently celebrated their 30th anniversary.

EXERCISE

1. Take 5 minutes each day to write out your feelings. If you don't know what you feel, write out any physical symptoms, e.g., "my neck is stiff; my shoulder is in knots." After a period of time you will associate the physical symptom with the feeling.

2. Once every hour, ask yourself what you are feeling. Don't do anything about it; just get in the habit of checking in with what you feel.

3. Before you go to bed, light a candle and stare at it for three minutes, concentrating on your breath.

4. John Stevens wrote a book on awareness that includes an exercise called *The Rosebush*:

- Close your eyes and imagine you are a rosebush.
- Where are you planted?
- Are you big or small?
- Do you have thorns?
- What do they look like?
- What color are you?
- Do you have many blossoms?
- Are your roots deep?
- What is around you? Other rosebushes? Are they like you? Are there different forms of vegetation? Are you alone?
- Is your soil rich or sandy?
- Who takes care of you?
- Describe yourself in each of the four seasons.
- Are you where you belong?

Take out a piece of paper and write in first person the answer to those questions, e.g., "I am a wild rose, high on a craggy hill," etc.

At the end of this exercise read your answers. They will reveal a lot of what you feel about your life and relationship.

CHAPTER 2

CLAIMING Your Role

Love, when I see your face it is mottled
Love, when I see your face it is blurred
Love, when I see your face I forget where I am
I no longer see your face
I no longer call you love

You and your partner brought many things to the relationship that you have created together. Many of those contributions served to strengthen the bond between you while others have, over time, pulled you apart. Before your relationship issues can be resolved, you must assess and claim all that you have contributed, both positive and negative. You need to understand the role you have played and how it developed.

TRIGGERS FROM THE PAST

A part of every past relationship continues to exist in your current union in the form of memories, preferences, and reactions. Unhealed wounds, resentment, and anger from the past can become part of the present when they are triggered by something your current partner says or does. You may not understand why you react so strongly, and your partner is likely to be equally confused by your reaction. Your behavior may even serve as a trigger for your partner's own past hurts.

Stored pain may be leftover from childhood, previous romantic relationships, or a myriad of other things. If, for example, you had unresolved issues with your father or mother, those wounds can seep into your love relationships. An argument that in a healthy relationship would be resolved through clear communication can turn into World War III when it triggers unmet needs and anger from a past relationship. It is no longer about you and your partner, but about you and your past, and your partner just gets caught in the crossfire. Because your partner doesn't understand the reason for the intensity of your reaction, tremendous hurt and confusion can result.

When I received the letter from graduate school telling me I had been accepted into the program, my husband held it high in the air above me so that I couldn't reach it. He was just teasing, but I became furious. Someone from my past had teased me mercilessly in the same manner, and I was really reacting to years of that person's taunting. But it was my husband who got the full force of my anger.

ASSESSING YOUR BEHAVIOR

The potential for misdirected anger makes it important to be very clear about everything you've brought into your relationships. One of my clinical supervisors told me that when you get into bed with your partner, you're sharing the bed with all of his or her previous partners (and family), along with your own. So the bed can get a little crowded! By examining past relationships and dealing with any unresolved issues, you'll create a lot more space in the bed for you and your partner.

Examining past relationships and assessing your behavior in them takes courage. You have to look in the mirror and ask, "What was my part in this? How did I help create the problems?" It's so much easier to blame the other person, especially when you've gotten a lot of sympathy from friends for all the injustice you suffered.

When I hear someone describe a pending breakup with phrases such "he is," "she did it again," "he won't," or "that greedy...," I know there is a long way to go. Please don't misunderstand. Anger is a real, legitimate, and necessary part of the process. Go ahead and be angry. Write out your feelings, telling your best friend what a bitch she is and your husband what an ungrateful bastard he is. Then get to the important part: it doesn't matter what he or she is. If you choose to end the relationship, the only person you will take with you is you. So work on yourself. Concentrate on what you can do differently. Change yourself so that you can change the things you did that added to the demise of your last relationship.

EXPECTATIONS

When you entered this union, were you prepared to do your part or did you instead expect your partner to make up for all your unmet needs from the past? Were you hoping this partner would bend over backwards to be perfect and make you safe from pain and struggle? Asking your partner to be perfect is akin to saying, "Don't be real; you and your needs are less important than mine."

If you think of yourself as a giving person who has understandably carried a little sensitivity from the past, it may come as a shock to be described as a controller who is manipulating the relationship for her benefit instead of building a relationship based on intimacy and love. But when you gain some clarity about your current situation, you may come to realize that your partner has tired of making up for your past wounds and has chosen to be authentic in his interactions with you. Now it's up to you to determine how you feel about this "real" individual and whether you want to remain with him as he truly is.

DROPPING YOUR BAGGAGE

Being in a relationship automatically carries the risk of being hurt. As difficult as it might be to face your contribution to the issues between you and your partner, it's critical for the health of not only your current relationship, but any you might have in the future. No matter what happens between you and your partner, your expectations, triggers, and old hurts will continue to affect you until they are completely resolved.

As you begin the work of healing past injuries and resentments, ask yourself, "Am I considerate? Do I compromise? Do I listen? Do I give? Do I give to myself? Do I ask for what I want?" We teach others how to treat us. If, in the past, you have accepted unacceptable behavior and you haven't asked for what you want, then you're likely to repeat that behavior pattern with every partner.

MAKING A CLEAR CHOICE

If you carry a lot of baggage, I recommend that you work through those issues fully before making the ultimate decision about whether to continue or end your current relationship. If the pain runs deep or if you have difficulty resolving past hurts, counseling may be helpful in healing the wounds.

Even after you have assessed your past and begun to deal with old hurts, you may still be left with significant problems in your relationship. But through the process of examining and claiming your contributions to the issues between you, you can make a clear choice as to whether you will stay or leave. And, whatever you decide, you will be able to act with love.

EXAMPLE 1

I know a couple who have been married for 54 years. Even more impressive than their relationship longevity is that they are as much in love now as they were when they started, if not more so. Each of them always has something nice to say about the other. Their comments don't reflect the narcissistic bragging that stems from seeing your partner as a reflection of you (e.g., "Did you know that Steve was first in his division of tennis? And did I tell you the church wants him to speak next Sunday?") They instead talk about behaviors. (e.g., "I was so touched that George washed my car. He really knows how to make me feel special." or "I don't know if I could have beat my opponent in the lawsuit without Hallie's support.") That kind of acknowledgment is sincere, heartwarming, and inspiring. That kind of support keeps relationships going strong.

EXAMPLE 2

Liz says that one of the worst things she does is ignore her own feelings. As a result, she deals with her husband Tim in a passive-aggressive way. When Tim doesn't offer a romantic gesture on special days (such as Valentine's day), Liz is hurt and sees his lapse as evidence that Tim doesn't love her. Instead of voicing her disappointment, Liz retaliates by burning his dinner or "forgetting" to wash his good-luck shirt before an important golf game. She engages in silent warfare that can only undermine and ultimately destroy the very thing she says she wants.

Liz could, instead, address Tim directly, saying, "It may seem silly, but I put a lot of stock in romantic, even schmaltzy, gestures like flowers and cards. I feel disappointed when you don't do those things." Addressing the situation can be risky. Liz may be ignored, laughed at, or rejected. But if she never states her case, Liz will continue to live in the midst of an emotional cold war. Giving Tim an opportunity to hear her also gives him a chance to change. If he ignores her feelings after she has made them clear, she'll know there are deeper issues to address in their relationship.

EXERCISE 1

Buy a copy of *The Artist's Way* and write the morning papers, as the author suggests. This will give you a great deal of insight into your own issues and your role in your life's circumstances. You will see the impact your parents had on you and how, perhaps unconsciously, you have carried that behavior forward or elicited the same behavior.

If you come from an alcoholic or dysfunctional family, I urge you to buy John Bradshaws *Healing the Shame that Binds You*. He offers several helpful suggestions and exercises.

I also encourage all clients to walk, run, do yoga, or engage in some other form of exercise. Physical activity boosts self esteem and helps you deal effectively with stress and anger. If you really want to get an A+ in therapy, I highly recommend meditation. I could not have gotten through some of the rough spots in my life without it.

EXERCISE 2

For each problem in your relationship, ask yourself, "What am I objecting to? What does this behavior touch off for me? What's my part?" The process of uncovering and resolving past issues can take weeks, months, or years, so be patient.

CHAPTER 3

CHANGING Your Behavior

So, love, let me see you clearly
Not through clouds of yesterday
Then hope arises that you might come
Into my arms once more.

The process I'm describing unfolds one step at a time, with each discovery building on the one before and every action creating a new response. As you grow in awareness, experiencing the nuances of what you truly feel, want, and need in your relationship, the process becomes a ripple that expands in ever increasing circles from the point at which it began. The natural outcome of this expanding awareness is a change in your behavior toward your partner as you work out your own part in the relationship.

TAKING OWNERSHIP OF YOUR BEHAVIOR

Before you can change any behavior, you must first become aware of what it is you're doing and why. Then you need to own that behavior, to acknowledge, at least inwardly, that you have final responsibility for everything you do and say.

If, for example, you know that you tend to misdirect your anger with an ex-spouse to your current partner, admit it first to yourself. Then, when you're ready, you'll be able to admit the misdirection to your partner, allowing the inner healing to show in your outward life. You might say, "I realize that I've been allowing myself to be triggered pretty easily. I'd like you to take the garbage out more often, but I don't want to lay the blame on you for things my ex-husband did. Could we talk about this?"

Even better, if you've resolved your issues with your ex by working with a therapist, you may reach a point when all you'll need to say is, "Hey, would you mind taking out the garbage?" without any overtones of blame or contempt. If your partner ignores your request, you can choose to handle it yourself or discuss the situation calmly and constructively.

If there is a lot of discord in your relationship and you've worked through some of the issues on your own, you may be ready to discuss your relationship openly. You might say to your partner, "I feel ready now. Can we talk about what's going on with us?" This may be a very scary moment, but it can represent a crucial turning point in your relationship.

When you do talk seriously with your partner about the issues between you, begin by discussing your part in the process. Admit the ways you've helped create the problems and share the behavior changes you're prepared to make. Focusing initially on your shortcomings allows your partner to let down his defenses and share constructive ideas for mutual change.

CHANGING YOUR PERCEPTIONS

If you have a romanticized view of love, mundane everyday schedules may lead you to believe the romance has disappeared from your relationship. If you can view having your partner unload the dishwasher voluntarily as a loving act on par with planning a candlelight dinner (one of my personal favorites), you will have expanded your perception of romance. By letting your partner know how much you appreciate his thoughtfulness, you will also deepen the aliveness of your relationship.

It's the little things that provide the glue in relationships. One of my friends, during a heated argument with the man she describes as the love of her life, asked him to leave. Three days later, she let him return. She admitted that she deeply missed the way he woke her every day by bringing her coffee in bed. His morning gesture was a small thing, but it was something that she didn't want to lose.

CHANGING YOUR BELIEF SYSTEMS

Closely related to your perceptions are your belief systems and attitudes. If your father's death when you were two years old has led you to believe that all men will abandon you, that belief might become a self-fulfilling prophecy. By clinging so tightly that your partner has no breathing room or by making yourself so unappealing that even a saint would want to escape, you virtually guarantee that your belief in abandonment will be confirmed. Or you may pick partners who are totally inappropriate. I had one date with a charming man who, I learned, had been married five times. His relationship track record made him the perfect candidate for a woman who needs to prove that all men will leave.

THE COURAGE TO CHANGE

"Holy cow. I not only have to look at my behavior, but now I have to be the one to change when that son-of-a-gun is drinking and spending the kids' college fund?" That's the attitude many people have when I suggest they improve their relationship by focusing on changing themselves rather than their partner. There is an organization called Al-Anon that is filled with people who, rather than concentrating on changing their partners, are busy looking at their part. Members meet to discuss ways to keep the focus on themselves rather than on the other person. It works.

Changing your behavior, your attitudes, and your belief system takes courage, which I believe is a major ingredient for success in any area of life. Know that you are as worthy of happiness as anyone else. Avoid the temptation to keep everyone at arm's length until you are pretty enough and successful enough, or until you have worked through every issue known to man to make you good enough to be loved. Perfectionism is simply a mind game that masks your fears. Of course you are afraid. Who wants to be hurt? But you also don't want to stay frozen on the sidelines, afraid to take a chance. Focus instead on the potential reward that awaits once you've gained enough courage to release your fears.

ACCEPT THE CHALLENGE TO CHANGE

Start with small changes. They often offer a big payback in terms of happiness and personal fulfillment. And know that changes in your own behavior can often influence your partner's behavior. When seen in this light, personal healing takes on a whole new significance since it can serve as the catalyst for change in your relationship.

If you want to find out just how much you can affect the relationship, along with putting your commitment to it to the test, I challenge you to spend a month acting as if this is the perfect person for you. Show your love and appreciation to your partner. Let him know what attracted you in the first place and what continues to draw you to him. Notice during that month whether your relationship dynamic begins to change. It may or may not. But it won't hurt to try, and you might experience something quite wonderful.

EXAMPLE 1

A couple came into my office with a common issue. The woman announced that her husband drank too much. The man looked at me and said, "I am never going to AA, and I am not quitting drinking." I replied, "Who asked you to?" His mouth dropped open.

Then I started talking to his wife about Al-Anon. I asked how the drinking was affecting her. She cried and talked about taking care of their baby by herself and how frightening it was when he drank too much. I asked her to come back by herself. She gradually learned to ignore his drinking and go ahead with plans she had made even if he wasn't available because he was drunk or late. She became more matter-of-fact about the situation and started making friends of her own.

Eventually, her husband asked to come to a session with her. This time, he looked at me and said, "Okay, you win. I'll go to AA. "I replied, "Okay, you win. You'll have your wife." He stopped by five years ago to say hello. He was still sober. And they had had two more children together.

EXAMPLE 2

In the *Awareness* section I talk about a couple whose marriage was in a deplorable state. After several months of sobriety and marriage counseling, the husband had to make a decision. He had had two affairs and there was some danger the truth would come out. He needed to decide whether to tell his wife himself or hope and pray that she wouldn't find out.

I sat quietly as he contemplated his dilemma. Finally, he looked up, ashen, and said, "Ask her to come in, please." He then admitted the affairs directly and simply. His wife was devastated.

As it turns out, she would have discovered his secret, and he had curtailed some of the pain by revealing the truth himself. Today she views him as her hero, and he knows that she has stood by him through the most terrible of storms. I am not saying that coming clean about something like an affair is never a deal breaker. In this case, however, the husband not only had the courage to reveal an unpleasant truth about himself, but he then worked tremendously hard to make sure he changed.

EXERCISE

Imagine that you've been given the power to become the person you most want to be. Describe that person in detail.

Now list 12 ways that the person you are now differs from the ideal you just described. How can you become more like the person you would like to be? What changes would be necessary?

Plan to adopt one change a month for the next year. Aim for excellence, but not perfection, as you make these changes.

CHAPTER 4

OVERCOMING Martyrdom & Abuse

My bones ache inside at the thought of my task
Let me run like a child and hide forever in my mother's arms
I turn my tearstained face, squinting a glimpse of my direction
Slowly I move toward my dread...my heart begins to open.

One of the hardest roles to drop is that of the victim, whether the role is real or imagined. People who are abused physically, sexually, and/or emotionally are the real victims. They become trapped in a downward spiral of poor self-worth, learned helplessness, pain, and despair. Abuse victims deserve our sympathy and need inspiration, hope, and support in order to change their circumstances.

Martyrdom is the habitual perception of victimization. A martyr may truly be a victim of abuse, but a sense of martyrdom can exist apart from any mistreatment. In the absence of abuse, the martyr magnifies every slight and focuses attention on the suffering he/she must endure. Abuse victims, on the other hand, tend to feel ashamed of their situation and may go to great lengths to hide the violence they experience.

OVERCOMING MARTYRDOM

While the term "victim" implies helplessness, playing the victim can actually be quite powerful. During group sessions, I sometimes ask a member to lie down on the floor. Then I ask the group where the attention is focused. Of course, all attention is on the person lying on the floor. At the moment, that one individual has all the power.

The seductiveness of the power inherent in the role of the "wronged one" is insidious. You may gain attention by putting up with someone else's poor behavior. You may like hearing, "Poor Jan. I don't know how she tolerates that man." And you may gain the secondary benefit of being able to guilt-trip the person you believe has wronged you, which offers an incredible amount of control. But in the long run, you're hurting yourself more than you know. Attention is a poor substitute for genuine closeness.

Martyrdom may have become an automatic part of your behavior if you see yourself as the poor victim who was left behind. You may use your pain to gain attention and control instead of accepting your part in what happened in past relationships and then using that knowledge to change. The age-old question, "Would you rather be right or be happy?" applies here. For a martyr, the need to be proven right can easily overcome the desire to be happy. Happiness is risky because it might not last. Being miserable may feel safer because there is no risk of falling from grace.

There are so many reinforcers for martyrdom in our society. Most of us have people in our lives who genuinely love us, but don't want things to change. If we think about divorce or starting a new relationship, these loving, well-meaning individuals may find a myriad of ways to keep the situation (and us) the same. Don't blame them, although it may be tempting. They feel threatened by and uncomfortable with the change in the air, so they subtly, and perhaps unconsciously, fight to keep things the same.

ABUSE

Physical abuse includes any kind of physical intimidation or the implied threat thereof. I have heard men say, "I have never hit a woman," and they believe that separates them completely from the issue of abuse. But they bang their fists on the table when they get angry or snarl "watch out" through clenched teeth. That kind of implied violence is, indeed, abuse. At the other end of the continuum, there are cases where the violence is so severe that either staying in the relationship or leaving it can place the person's life in danger.

No one should initiate or accept abuse. If you are experiencing abuse, the situation may be too highly charged for change to happen gradually, so it's likely that healing will need to occur outside the relationship. The first goal for anyone being abused must be safety, which usually means removing yourself from the abusive situation. From a place of safety, explore (perhaps with a counselor who has expertise in abuse recovery) how you became involved in that dynamic and what steps you might take to ensure it doesn't happen in future relationships.

Protecting yourself from abuse certainly doesn't mean avoiding relationships altogether. Unfortunately, many people do just that. They avoid intimacy by gaining weight, succumbing to depression, becoming workaholics, or indulging in promiscuous sex. But giving your power away by denying yourself love and happiness is not the answer. You deserve to be safe. You deserve to be happy. You deserve to be loved.

We are taught, and rightfully so, to be kind and giving and loving. But we're seldom cautioned about depleting ourselves in the process. We should be taught not to cross the line where getting our needs met becomes secondary. If you have crossed that line, it's time to turn around and go back to the place where your needs are as important as those of anyone else in your life.

EXAMPLE 1

Verbal abuse often transforms, in time, into emotional abuse that involves guilt tripping, shaming, and demeaning. For example, one woman confessed to her husband she had had an affair. Although she had rebuffed most of his attempts at intimacy for years, she blamed her husband for driving her to have an affair, claiming that she turned to another man because her husband had stopped approaching her. She saw herself as the victim, minimizing her own role in the situation.

EXAMPLE 2

When you choose to change, you may be judged instead of being supported. You might be confronted with variations of, "How could you leave him when he was down and out?" One client decided to stand up for herself and responded to that question with, "Well, he's been looking for a job for ten years and I finally got it that being down and out WAS his job."

EXERCISE 1

Give your partner the opportunity to react differently by dropping any tendencies toward martyrdom. Rather than nagging about the TV being on all the time, simply state that you prefer not to watch at that moment. Then go read a book or do something else you enjoy. Find multiple, healthy ways to get your needs met rather than blaming the other person for stifling you. Instead of objecting to things you don't like, make changes designed to give you both what you need and want.

EXERCISE 2

If you are the abuser, please seek appropriate counseling. In the meantime, take a look at the way you deal with anger. Chances are great that you feel frightened by confrontation and avoid it most of the time. When the anger builds, however, it can spill over into rage. You may begin by attacking other people verbally, perhaps through sarcasm, which is an indirect way of masking anger. If you often find yourself saying, "Oh, I was just kidding" or "You're just too sensitive," you may have an anger problem and be engaging in a form of abuse.

CHAPTER 5

CONFRONTING Your Partner

How can I speak when I tremble with fear
What can I say so you know what I feel
How can I possibly share what might wound us?
Forgive me because the silence is far worse.

Just as it takes two people to create a relationship, it takes two to heal one when problems arise. As we discussed in previous sections, you can start the healing process by becoming aware of – and changing – your own behavior. But at some point, your partner will need to make changes, too. That step may require confrontation.

It's a big step, but by letting your partner know you are dissatisfied with the relationship, you allow the relationship to progress. However, even if you found it relatively easy to work on your own issues, you may be tempted to bypass this important step. Some people sidestep confrontation to avoid hurting their partner's feelings. Others consider confrontation unnecessary because they're sure it's already obvious to their partners that they're unhappy. That's seldom the case. I have worked with hundreds of people in therapy who have experienced profound, seemingly endless dissatisfaction while their partners had only a minutia of an idea how deep it went. When confronted with the truth, those formerly unaware partners were stunned.

Of course, you may avoid confrontation because you fear giving your partner the heads up that not only are you dissatisfied, but you aren't sure the relationship can be fixed. By revealing the truth about your feelings, you may be rocking your own boat and creating a higher level of uncertainty. Once the other person realizes the extent of your unhappiness, he might take control and make the decision to end the relationship. If you haven't resolved your feelings about whether or not you want the relationship to end, that can be very frightening.

For many of us, confrontation in general is scary. Clients tell me that they're just not good at confronting. "It's just not my thing," they say. "I've tried it before and it makes things worse."

All the potential reasons for avoiding confrontation involve valid concerns. Your partner's feelings may be hurt; he may already sense your dissatisfaction and be unmoved by it; and, if your partner is already unhappy in the relationship, confrontation may prompt him to leave. And if you aren't comfortable with confrontation under the best of circumstances, it will certainly be difficult for you to do it now. But you only have two other options: (1) keep things as they are and continue to be unhappy or (2) end the relationship without giving your partner a chance to change.

MY PATH TO CONFRONTING

I completely understand how difficult confrontation can be. People tend to view me as someone who confronts easily and well. And after many years of practice, it may be true that I confront effectively. But it's never easy.

When I first became aware of my need to learn confrontation skills (also termed "assertiveness"), I was filled with dread. I would agonize over the issue for a long time and then proceed to scare the daylights out of the person I was about to confront by saying with deadly seriousness, "I need to talk to you." No one likes to feel they've been called into the principal's office for a scolding. The reactions I got after confronting ranged from, "For a minute, I thought our friendship was over" to " Why you didn't just say so earlier?"

Eventually, I became more at ease with talking about my feelings and able to do so without a heavy or judgmental tone, which made it easier for the other person to hear me. Of course, it's much less challenging for me to confront when working with clients. However, in my personal life, I face all the fears that you face. I'm more emotionally involved, so it can be difficult to remain matter-of-fact. But it can be done.

It's not necessary to express every concern and confront every situation that pops up. I recommend that you develop a sense of timing and discretion when it comes to sharing your views. That may sound hard to do, but I discovered that as I trusted my integrity in speaking up for myself more and more, I found it easier to let most things go without commenting on them.

When you do choose to confront, do so gently and be aware of the distinction between confronting and accusing. Accusations put the other person on the defensive. The walls come up and communication breaks down. So instead of making your partner's behavior wrong, in general, tell him why it's wrong *for you*. That requires "I" language. When you're tempted to say, "You never help out around the house," substitute "I feel overwhelmed by all the work that has to be done around the house and would like to brainstorm ways we could work together to get it done." Gentle confrontation, combined with a request, opens the lines of communication and invites your partner to contribute to a joint resolution.

If you continue to find yourself balking at the prospect of confrontation, consider the possibility that confronting your partner could serve as a catalyst to help you create a new, more loving relationship that is built on communication, collaboration, and mutual respect. Even if the relationship ultimately ends, you will know you did everything you could to give healing a chance. It's worth the risk.

EXPRESSING APPRECIATION

It may seem strange to discuss appreciation alongside confrontation, but they are flip sides of the communication coin...and for many people they are equally difficult to accomplish, especially when relationship problems have created so many obstacles. If, however, you can learn to pair confronting with lots of positive feedback, you're likely to experience better results than if all you do is confront your partner. What you say doesn't have to be complicated. "Thank you for calling to let me know you were running late. I really appreciated it." That's all it takes.

When my father died, I was a teenager. For a few years, our relationship had taken a beating, but we became very close during the last year of his life. We enjoyed many special moments, and I told him shortly before he died how much I loved him and how proud of him I was. Thirty years later, I still feel gratitude for whatever wisdom prompted me to share my feelings with him before it was too late.

Pursuing the illusion of safety by withholding love and refusing to appreciate your partner's good qualities and behaviors keeps you from experiencing the full richness of life. Let go. Allow yourself to confront gently and appreciate freely. Express who you are. Be available, open, and honest so your partner doesn't have to guess where you're coming from.

I challenge you to express yourself fully in every relationship. If time runs out before you've expressed your love or joy for the people in your life or cleared up old resentments, how will you feel? Don't leave unfinished business. Don't put yourself in the position of writhing with regret. Instead, toward the end of each day, check in with yourself to be sure you've said what you wanted to say and done what you wanted to do in your relationships.

EXAMPLE

A woman who expected her husband to know what she wanted spent several unhappy years believing he didn't love her. Every Friday night, he would come home from work and ask her what she wanted to do that evening. She thought he didn't care enough to come up with ideas on his own, so she would respond, "I don't know."

The truth was that her father-in-law had been very domineering and seldom gave his wife a choice in a decision. Her own husband wanted to treat his wife with more respect and love than his mother had been given. To him, that meant letting his wife decide.

After a year of counseling she worked up the courage to say, "When you ask me what I want to do, I feel as though you don't care about me. If you did, you would know what I like and would come up with a plan." The simple phrase "when you…, I feel" can clear up a myriad of misunderstandings and hurt feelings.

In return, her husband explained where he was coming from and they laughed and cried together. It's a bit like O'Henry's tale of the man who sold his watch to buy combs for his wife's hair. She had cut her hair and sold it to buy him a watch chain.

EXERCISE

You may read about the couple in the example above and think, "Well, I wouldn't be afraid to talk about that." But there's probably some topic that you don't feel comfortable addressing with your partner.

Answer the following questions:
- What are you afraid to talk about and what feelings have you stuffed?
- Do you feel free, always, to say what you want and need to say?
- When was the last time you told your partner about something that hurts or bothers you?

CHAPTER 6

ALLOWING Space for Change

Your breath is yours
I want it to match mine
Stay in the shallows
My soul yearns for the deep.

Through this process, you've become aware of the issues in your relationship and your part in them; you're changing your own behaviors; and you've gotten past your fears and confronted your partner. Now what? Now you allow change to happen. In other words, you wait.

GIVE YOUR PARTNER A CHANCE

By the time you've reached the confrontation stage, you've already begun the process of change. It's only fair that you give your partner an equal chance to change. Unfortunately, most of us are impatient. Even if we've delayed working through our own issues for years, it's tempting to rush things once we've confronted our partner. We'd rather have a painful absolute than live with ongoing uncertainty. "This is too scary," you may think. "I know it's not going to work. I just want to know it's over so I can get on with my life."

Instead of a giving your partner a chance, you give him an ultimatum: "You have half an hour to clean up your act, or I'm out of here." Or you may bypass ultimatums in favor of becoming your partner's personal monitor. In effect, you say to your partner, "I've told you want I want and need. Let's check in and see if you're changing." No one can effectively change or explore or view things from a better perspective when he's under a microscope. After awhile, most people feel so pressured by close observation and implied criticism that they lose interest in changing altogether. At that point, it's much easier to walk away than to try to heal the relationship.

RELEASING CONTROL

It's a control issue. And while attempts to control don't work at any point in a relationship, at this stage they can spell disaster. This is a make-it or break-it situation in which the outcome of the relationship will be determined. As frustrating as it may be, you need to completely release control. If you have to force your partner to behave in a certain way in order for you to be happy, what will happen when the pressure is removed? It's likely the situation will return to the way it was when you started this whole process. It may be even worse. It certainly won't be transformed into a replica of the time when your love was fresh and new.

That man who bent down to sweetly kiss me years ago on a San Francisco street corner might want very different things now. And I'm no longer the girl with long blond hair and flowers on her coat. Those images of the past claimed their moments, but each of us had the right to change and become who we now are.

ACCEPTANCE AND APPRECIATION

I believe we need to accept each other as we are in this moment. If your partner loves tennis, for example, it may have become an important part of his life because it meets many of his needs. So he plays every weekend. You might ask for a compromise in terms of frequency, but you must accept that tennis is part of who your partner is. Somehow it was part of the equation that initially attracted you to him.

You may not be able to embrace certain aspects of another person, and that's OK. Deal breakers come in many forms. But trying to change your partner is likely to backfire. Even if his behavior changes for awhile, he's likely to resent you. And something special in your relationship will be lost.

Once you become comfortable with the natural process of change, you can release control and remember the past and the love it held without being attached to the people you used to be...or the person you want the other to become. Then you might be able to say to your partner, "Let me see if I can grow enough to trust your feelings for me without a need to have you prove them over and over."

UNCERTAINTY AND DETACHMENT

Deepok Chopra says that the highest spiritual state involves existing within the law of uncertainty. Faith grows when you don't know what's going to happen. But human beings sometimes crave certainty so much that we will end a relationship prematurely rather than allowing our partner time to change. Waiting patiently in the midst of uncertainty takes great courage.

Courage is a concept that has been largely ignored in the realm of psychology. But courage is exactly what it takes to look inside yourself and become aware of your part in relationship issues. It also takes courage to reveal to your partner the depth of your dissatisfaction. And it requires courage to wait for a change in the other that might never come. But if you can find that courage, great healing can occur.

Living with uncertainty requires the detachment that comes from deep spiritual maturity. Detachment arises from the ability to go to a quiet, calm place and find the inner resource of trust within yourself. In order to be detached, you must do what you need to do to take care of yourself and you must allow the other person to do the same.

It can be very difficult to allow a person for whom you may currently feel little affection the opportunity to decide without pressure. You may be aware in every minute that the changes that person chooses to make could end your relationship. Maintaining a sense of detachment under these circumstances will test your resolve and push you to the limit, but if you succeed, you will have gained the priceless gifts of self mastery and inner trust.

EXAMPLE

After my client confessed to his wife that his excessive drinking had been accompanied by multiple affairs, both of them had to allow the other time to change.

Before she learned of the affairs, his wife had been patient, allowing her husband time to get his alcoholism under control. Once he confessed the affairs, it was his turn to wait. He allowed her the space to decide whether or not she could stay in the relationship despite her feelings of betrayal. It was a painful time for both of them. He remained steady and loving, not knowing whether she would ever be able to forgive him.

Initially, she was devastated, angry, righteous, and unforgiving. For two years he did not know what the outcome was going to be. He listened as she expressed her anger, and he continued to work on himself to understand his behavior. He did his best to forgive himself and remain strict in his attendance at A.A. meetings. After a lot of work and much healing, she was able to forgive him and remain in the marriage.

The couple was, in the end, able to repair an almost irreparable situation.

My belief is that if he hadn't been addicted, she would not have forgiven him. But his alcoholism and his determination to overcome it gave her both an understanding of the reasons for the affairs and trust that he could change.

EXERCISE 1

Think back to the time when your relationship was new. What attracted you to your partner then? Do those qualities still exist in him? If so, do you continue to appreciate the qualities that once captivated you?

EXERCISE 2

Waiting patiently is easier when you are taking excellent care of yourself. What are some things you can do to feel nurtured? What activities do you enjoy that you haven't done lately? Indulge yourself. Make yourself feel special. You'll find that the time passes quickly and you'll be better prepared to accept whatever happens in your relationship.

CHAPTER 7

OPENING Yourself

Trembling, I steel myself to hear words that I want to say
belong to another
Must I endure insults and pain
when it would be so much easier to run?
Who are you to sit in judgment?
Perhaps you are the angel who leads me to love,
and your name, my dear, is truth.

After you have confronted your partner and allowed him space to change, there may come a time when he will be ready to return the favor by confronting you. It can be a challenging time. Most of us don't do as well when we're sitting in the hot seat as we do when we're the ones turning up the heat. But great progress can be made, both on a relationship and a personal level if you can fully open yourself to hearing what your partner has to say.

You won't agree with all of it and you don't have to. Some points may have validity, while others will be misdirected. Listen to it all, the welcome and the unwelcome, the true and the blatantly false. A psychologist once commented that it's easy to label your teenage daughter rebellious when she consistently calls you a witch with a capital "B." But maybe you should pay attention. It's possible she is seeing in you qualities you would like to change if you could see them for yourself.

One of the most effective forms of therapy takes place in a group where you gain the perspective of strangers who don't have an investment in seeing you in a certain way. It is difficult to see ourselves through others eyes, and even more difficult to understand the impact we have on others. If we don't take personal responsibility for how we impact the people in our lives, we can continue to behave however we wish. The price for this denial is the risk of making the same mistakes and, thus, continuing to create dysfunctional relationships.

Every person in your life can serve as a mirror and a teacher. Listen closely and remain open to seeing yourself as others see you. You might stumble onto something that can help you change your life for the better. So take it all in. In fact, invite feedback from your partner – the more, the better.

Accepting negative feedback graciously and using it constructively takes courage. You must be able to put your ego aside and relinquish your need to be right all the time. But beware the tendency to own everything without examining it carefully. It can be tempting to say, "It's all my fault. I did everything wrong." But that's just another way of retaining control and avoiding the need to be the learner, the one who needs to change. Instead, strive for a healthy balance between admitting that you've done everything wrong and insisting that you're 100% in the right.

At this stage, you might consider therapy, either together or separately. I typically recommend that couples do some individual work first so that each can be clear about where his/her own issues end and the relationship problems begin. Whether or not your partner agrees to participate, it's important to take care of yourself through counseling or some other form of support.

Opening requires that you lower your defenses after what may be years of anger, hurt, and pain. The risk is that you will be disappointed once more. What is so easy to miss is that even if it turns out differently from the way you hope, you will have learned to do your part. That makes you much more likely to connect in a future relationship. A friend of mine frequently says, "What the other person does is none of my business." That shows a very high level of spiritual achievement. If I'm able to feel a little of that from time to time, I know that my growth is in high gear.

As a therapist, I wholeheartedly believe in therapy. I've seen it work and I've experienced the benefits personally. Having an objective supporter is immensely helpful in guiding you through the process of healing. It can make a very difficult journey much easier and less painful. But I always honor the individual's process and the choice each person makes as to the best way to travel the path ahead.

EXAMPLE 1

The advantages of being open are relevant to all relationships, including romances, friendships, business, and families. Our attitude holds tremendous power. When we release needless hurt and anger, we remove many of the reasons for others to react negatively to us.

I worked with a mother who had a long history of clashing with her daughter. They had finally worked through many of their differences, but were still a little tentative in relating to each other. On a visit to my office, the mother admitted feeling hurt by her daughter's attitude about something that meant a lot to her. Old assumptions and resentments raced through her mind, and she felt discouraged.

Then she decided to focus on the positive things that were happening in her life and her relationship with her daughter. Once she let go of her own tension, there were no longer any bad feelings that her daughter could reflect back to her. The response was almost immediate. Her daughter became sunny, happy, and loving.

EXAMPLE 2

I often wonder how many people have gotten divorced or never married in the first place simply because they are too frightened to let someone in. That was the case with a beautiful 35-year-old woman who came to see me. She had been blessed with good looks and brains. She had a good job and was spiritually centered and healthy. A divorcee, she attracted men like crazy. But she seldom met men she could genuinely care for and, when she did, they were either unavailable or clearly not in her league. Although she has had therapy in the past and probably needs more, she certainly is not a basket case.

Her parents are divorced and she has just one memory of doing something alone with her dad. It's interesting that in therapy she has worked on every issue except her distance from her father. She insists she cannot get in touch with any feelings of anger toward him. But when she meets men, she tests and retests them, and I am convinced she would refuse to even consider a man who would treat her well. That would require a level of openness that might challenge her in unaccustomed (and frightening) ways.

EXERCISE

This is a relatively simple, but quite powerful, exercise. For one day, look each person in the eye and take a moment to say something sincere. For example, when you walk into your office, make eye contact with your secretary and tell her you honestly did not like the report she completed. Then ask her what you can do to help her improve it.

Next, reverse the scenario by saying something positive. When you eat lunch at a restaurant, look directly at the waitress and let her know how much you appreciate her remembering that you take cream with your coffee.

The point of these exercises is to be open, which may or may not mean being positive. Do this for an entire day, then write down your reactions and how you feel, in general, at the end of the day.

CHAPTER 8

ACCEPTING the Ending

I long for my anger, for my pain
With their release, I am left with gentle sadness
As they flew away they took what I clung to
That is all that was left – love, we are done

Acknowledging that a relationship is troubled creates a point of no return. You can never completely reclaim the state of either innocence or denial that once allowed you to be oblivious to the issues between you. This forms a crossroads at which you and your partner must decide which way to go. Either the relationship will move forward...or you and your partner will move on with separate lives.

A continuing challenge for me both professionally and personally is that so many people want to quit instead of going for the full enchilada. They could have a better relationship, a better job, a better life by just releasing the desire to control and taking a few chances. Equally frustrating it the opposite tendency to stick with the known, even it it's painful, rather than taking the risk to change their lives.

I used to want every client who came to me to become self-actualized and reach his or her fullest potential. What a pain-in-the-neck therapist I was! I had to learn that for some just a small improvement is more than ample, and that each of us has the right to decide how far we want to stretch. When a woman who is married to an alcoholic makes peace with the fact that none of her needs will be met inside the relationship and decides to stay anyway, we may be shocked. You may ask, as I did, "Why stay when you can go out into the world and find greater happiness?" But in the end, it is her right, and no one else is qualified to determine what is best for her. On the other hand, we need not be limited by her decision. We, too, have the right to follow our own hearts even when they tell us to risk it all and go for the brass ring.

So if your inner voice tells you it's over, the time has come to let go. That point in time may arise after much soul searching, communication, and therapy, or it may come at the end of a pleasant weekend away with your partner. Although you enjoyed some very nice moments and effectively changed a few patterns, you just know deep inside that the relationship has reached the end. It may have nothing at all to do with your partner. It's not about blame, but about what you can live with. You know you've done everything you could do, tried all you could try, and you're simply, undeniably done. You'll recognize that moment when it happens.

My moment of acceptance arrived unexpectedly on a really rough day. I now see that I was in a relationship that I was destined to leave from the beginning. I did, however, have the opportunity this time to leave in a much healthier way than I'd left my marriage years earlier. When my marriage fell apart, I didn't know how to end with love. But I was given a second chance to exit a relationship with grace. I am so grateful for that experience. The steps I am sharing with you are the very steps I used to give that relationship a chance to heal and the steps that, ultimately, allowed me to end with love instead of bitterness.

When I told my partner that it was time for me to end the relationship, there was no arguing or drama. Because we had both prepared for this step, we were able to part with very little confrontation. Accomplishing that kind of acceptance requires exquisite listening as you progress through the steps of awareness, lack of blame, and patience. You must be able to confront your partner – and yourself – in a balanced way. But you need to wait until your inner clock tells you the time is right. That takes a lot of patience because the temptation is often to bail as soon as you know things aren't going well. Timing is crucial.

The result of great timing can be an ending that is more matter-of-fact than dramatic. That result is what you're likely to get when you've done your part in ending the relationship so thoroughly and lovingly that acceptance is complete.

EXAMPLE

The moment when you know you are done…or when you know you are going to stay is a moment most of us will remember forever. For me, a quiet resignation follows, and I make plans to go on with my life. If my decision is to leave, I begin to share less as I recognize it really doesn't matter anymore.

Jane was in a relationship that had had some severe problems, but her partner desperately wanted her and promised he would do anything to make it work. His apparent sincerity touched her, so she decided to give it a little more time. Then one day a friend called and asked if they had broken up. "Not really," she said, and she explained the situation. Her friend informed Jane that her partner was advertising on a computer dating service.

Jane checked it out, then confronted her partner. His defensiveness and anger told her the truth. "I'm done," she thought. It no longer mattered what he did. Their relationship was over.

EXERCISE

Think back to a relationship that ended in the past. It can be a friendship, romance, or work relationship. Did you end it or did the other person? When did you know that the relationship was over and how did you feel about the prospect of parting? What was your level of acceptance at the end?

The answers to these questions can provide insight into some of the issues you may have with relationships. That awareness can help you develop better coping skills that will allow you to create healthier relationships in the future – and to leave more gracefully, if leaving becomes the best option.

CHAPTER 9

LEAVING Gracefully

I saw a shadow fall across my path
If I turned a different direction
Sunlight chased it away

When a relationship ends, it can happen quietly or in the midst of emotional chaos. The resulting climate has a lot to do with how thoroughly you've prepared and the level of acceptance that has been reached by each partner. There's no foolproof way, however, of predicting whether a breakup will be amicable or hostile. All parties might be pleasant and cooperative or the gloves may come off...and either response can come as a surprise.

One of my clients was married to a man who had a history of being verbally abusive. So when she decided to leave him, she expected fireworks. Instead, he finally got it. He did a total turnaround and was as gentle as a lamb. They got along better after the divorce than they ever did as husband and wife. And I was as surprised as his wife at this happy turn of events.

But the threat of divorce can also bring out the worst in people. Once all hope of reconciliation is gone, you may see an unpleasant side of your partner that you never experienced before. I've witnessed nice guys and easygoing women turn very nasty as a divorce progresses. Whether your partner reacts to the split with grace or animosity, remember that your task is to leave the relationship spiritually as well as physically. You want to emerge from this life-altering event with honor and self-respect and, if possible, you want to help your partner do the same.

My belief is that ending a relationship doesn't result in bad karma, but leaving dishonorably can. So do your part by being fair to both you and your partner. If you have reached the stage of deep awareness and have done the other steps thoroughly so that you aren't placing blame, being fair will be relatively easy. However, anything can trigger a fight, and the division of property is a common trigger. Guard against overreacting when this happens and keep in mind your desire to leave the relationship in a state of spiritual wholeness.

Of course, you might grow so weary of the process that you just want the breakup to be over. Don't allow your desire for resolution to lead you to martyrdom. Stand up for yourself when the situation or your partner is unfair. At the opposite end of the continuum, you might find yourself hanging on when you need to let go. I'm familiar with one case in which the wife took her husband to court eight times. It wasn't about the money; she just couldn't let go of the marriage.

It is a kindness for everyone concerned, including the partners and the children (whether young or grown) to pull the trigger so that new lives can begin. Children may want things to stay the same, but they have as much need for acceptance and forward movement as everyone else. We all have to face the decision at some point whether to let go or hang on to a situation. When you release your relationship, you become a role model for your children. They will come out of the relationship breakup just fine even if they need to adjust in ways they never imagined.

When a relationship ends, no one really wins. Be thorough, then cut your losses and move forward with your life. Inevitably, the partner who carried most of the responsibility during the marriage will carry most of the responsibility in the divorce (and probably be dubbed the "bad guy" in the process). But don't let that stop you from making the decision you know you must.

The decision to leave comes down to knowing yourself and what you want from life. At what point do you say "enough"? What is the price of your freedom? Be aware of your desire and your needs. Be fair, be honest, be true, and then let go.

EXAMPLE

The actual physical act of tearing down a structure built for two and dividing things can be a difficult process. But if the parting is amicable, it can be accomplished relatively easily by turning it into a simple business transaction. Of course, both partners may not be in the same place.

The more a person is willing to let go of the past, the easier this stage will be. I am likely to say "keep the stuff," but there is some prudence in taking care of yourself and asking for what is important to you.

This may be a time of great elation. One client found a rental that was attractive. He went shopping and bought all new furniture and everything else he needed to set up housekeeping in his new place. He was like a kid in a candy store, getting to choose what he wanted for the first time in his life.

EXERCISE

Whether you're leaving or staying in the home you shared, go through each room and let the memories come. If certain rooms hold special memories, say what you need to say in order to silence the ghosts of the past. At the end of your sojourn take any cards, pictures, and other mementos that you no longer want in your life and get rid of them. Burn them or tear them into bits...whatever works for you. Read poetry or create a ritual if it feels right. Do whatever is meaningful for you to signify the ending of the old and the beginning of the new.

Then, begin your new life in your new space. If you're keeping the house the two of you lived in together, I recommend redecorating at least the bedroom. You're starting a new life, and your surroundings should reflect the change.

CHAPTER 10

GRIEVING the Loss

Blanketed in sweat-soaked sheets, I see 3am
No calling, nothing to distract me from the emptiness
There was a time when I ran to be by your side
4am will come and maybe tomorrow I will find peace
Sometime, perhaps, a new dream

Any major loss requires a grieving process. Whether the loss brings with it a sense of relief or sadness, it represents the ending of something you once valued greatly. The grieving may actually begin long before the relationship ends, but it accelerates rapidly once the ending is final. It's vitally important at that point to allow yourself time to grieve fully and completely. It's a lesson I learned late in the game.

In the past, my approach to any painful experience was to get very, very busy. When my first relationship ended, I threw myself into work in an insane way. It was an unsuccessful attempt to avoid feeling the pain of the grief I was experiencing deep in my soul. As a result, the grief process was prolonged and it took years for me to feel fully healed.

When another relationship ended a few years later, I was determined to handle it differently. I gave myself time alone. I gave myself the gift of gentleness. I wrote in my journal, walked, spent time with friends, and indulged in massages. I sat quietly in nature, reorganized my home, and gradually cleansed the ghost of lost love. I was so nurturing with myself.

Most importantly, I experienced my emotions. I allowed myself to get angry and feel the pain and then, when I was ready, I was able to gently let it go. Sometimes I slid into blame and condemnation. I knew, though, it was just my bruised ego seeking retribution. It's natural as a human being to have those feelings. They pose little problem when you see them for what they are and let them pass through you without acting on them.

During grief, you can experience mood swings ranging from elation to despair. You may have the sense that you could conquer the world and a few minutes later want to crawl into a corner and hide. When you're going through the process of grieving, I recommend that you read *How to Survive the Loss of a Love* by Harold H. Bloomfield, M.D. and Peter McWilliams. It has proven to be helpful for many of my clients and is short enough to be read even when you are deeply distressed.

In her definitive book *On Death and Dying*, Elisabeth Kubler-Ross described the stages of grief: denial, bargaining, anger, depression, and acceptance. Those stages apply as much to the ending of your relationship as they do to the death of someone you love. Your relationship has, indeed, died and it can be an enormous loss. Use your grieving time to meditate, write, exercise, and nurture yourself. Consider joining a support or therapy group to ease your passage through this painful process, especially if you find yourself hanging on too long.

Grief has a funny way of popping up in unexpected ways. A lovely woman was driving home three years after a divorce when she felt something on her cheek. She reached up to brush it away and realized that she was crying. She went home and sobbed. I call these healing tears. Even though you feel the pain as fully as in the early stages of grief, you can sense the difference in these tears, and the experience becomes a wonderful release. If she had tried to figure out what had triggered the tears, the healing process would have stopped prematurely. Just trusting where you are and allowing the completeness of your experience is incredibly cathartic.

The seeds of healing are watered by tears, so it's important to let the depression come and feel the pain of knowing your relationship is done. But this is a tough stage! While you may understand on an intellectual level that this is a time of transition, you may feel as if nothing will ever be good again. There is no hope on the horizon, and the prospect of new beginnings is something you can't comprehend. But after you dive into the depression and explore all of the painful feelings thoroughly, you do start to see the light again. Once you are able to say goodbye to whatever relationship you are hanging onto, you can emerge from your hypnotic trance and open yourself to life.

The process begins gradually as you become aware of simple pleasures: how the warm sun feels on your face, the deep purple of a flower, or the purr of a kitten. You notice the living things around you because you yourself are beginning to live again. You have fully embraced grief and allowed it to move through you. You can once more breathe and smile and feel the lightness of hope. Your rebirth has begun.

EXAMPLE 1

One of my clients had been married to a psychiatrist who left her after 25 years. She could not accept the divorce and took him back to court 8 times, even though he had remarried. She was stuck in anger. She felt her life had been ruined and, in fact, it was. But the person responsible for the ruin was my client because she chose not to move on.

EXAMPLE 2

Sometimes it can take years to obtain closure. A client who had been married to a naval submarine officer made love to her husband one morning before he went to work. Later that day his sub was destroyed and she never saw him again. For thirty years, even though she knew he was dead (and she had remarried), she felt as though he were just away on another mission. Due to the circumstances of his death, she hadn't seen his body or been able to visit his grave. So I asked her to go to Arlington and say goodbye. She fought me for quite awhile, but she finally did what I asked. She came back and told me, "I know he is dead." The freedom she gained allowed her to find a good relationship after her second marriage failed (which came as no surprise to me). Today, she is quite content.

EXERCISE

Close your eyes and imagine the person you are letting go (or the person you are having trouble releasing). See yourself connected to each other by a ribbon. What color is the ribbon? The intensity of the color gives you a clue. How much are you still connected and in what way? A red ribbon, for example, usually signifies anger.

Now see yourself cutting the ribbon. What happens to the other person after the ribbon has been severed? What happens to you? Your reaction may offer some clues about what still connects you.

Finally, see yourself turning quietly and walking away from your former partner without looking back.

CHAPTER 11

AWAKENING at Last

Angelic breath fills my lungs
I am gifted with another chance
Oh, a new life filled with possibility and laughter
I hear a chorus; tears sting my eyes
I have awakened from the dead

Endings and beginnings, by their very nature, happen simultaneously. But when you're in the midst of grief after a relationship has ended, there is little hope in the beginning of a life alone. Slowly, however, as you begin to heal, you feel it...the awakening of your spirit to a new and, if you've done your preparation thoroughly, richer life than you've ever experienced.

The awakening is about embracing life. You notice the world around you and see things that escaped your awareness before. I noticed ducks, birds, and beautiful flowers. You may be captivated by something entirely different. The nature of the awakening is unique to each individual, but it is always a sign that you are opening to life and moving on.

As I awakened, I began to challenge myself regularly to try new things. Yoga served as a majestic awakening for me that truly changed my life as much as therapy did. Today, I remain hungry for learning and life, even welcoming some of the discomfort because I know it is stimulating me. This is the stage where doors open, sunlight pours in, and we have the opportunity to be fully alive.

It's valuable at this time to turn around and look at the man or woman you were through all the stages you passed through on your way to this point. Give that past you a hug and kiss (or a thumbs-up if that feels more comfortable). Acknowledge the integrity, strength, and courage it took to do what you have done. Your willingness to go to the deepest part of your pain was incredibly courageous.

You have earned the joy you are beginning to feel as you emerge into this new existence. You are beautiful. You are brand new. You're wiser and more elegant. You bring with you not just the apple blossoms of springtime but the deep love of the earth, of depth, of knowledge. Your roots go deep.

Allow yourself to celebrate and express who you are. Be creative as you thank yourself and your friends for all the support they have given you. Practice gratitude and joy. Allow yourself to experience wonder. Ask yourself often, "What do I feel like doing?" Indulge in play and fun activities. Begin to set goals again, and enjoy the anticipation of wonderful adventures ahead. Know that you deserve all the good that you can dream of. Let yourself be happy. It is good to finish the grief, to laugh and love, perhaps this time more fully.

You have moved out of the darkness and into the sunlight, carrying with you all the beauty of the moonlit shadows through which you traveled. In yoga there is an expression at the end of each class. *Namaste* means "the divine in me salutes the divine in you." To all of you who have passed through these stages on your way to a beautiful present, I say, "Namaste."

EXAMPLE 1

Awakening is the most miraculous phase in the process that I've been describing. It is similar to recovering from a terrible illness. It can truly be a springtime in your life as your sense of aliveness returns and the world becomes filled with possibilities.

A woman left her abusive, alcoholic husband after 35 years. She packed a few belongings, got into her car, and left. For a long time, she was stalked by her husband, condemned by her family, and hounded in every way. She worked long hours for little money. But after years of pain and hard work, she emerged as a woman of beauty and grace. She owns her home and is in love with a man 12 years her junior. Her health has blossomed and she looks closer to his age than hers. She is filled with joy. Now she spends her evenings listening to her partner play the piano instead of watching her former husband drink himself into a stupor. She wept for joy as she told her therapy group that she likes to go to bed early so she and her new partner can hold each other and share the closeness of mutual love. "I never knew this was possible," she said, smiling through her tears.

EXAMPLE 2

It is not unusual during the awakening process for people to totally change the direction of their lives. A man who had gotten sober and worked through his grief in giving up his substance became aware of how much he disliked his job. He was the top administrator at a hospital, and his job was eating him alive. In therapy, he got clear about the effect his job was having on the other areas of his life and took a sabbatical. He used the time well, returning to school and earning a degree in a different area. He eventually quit his administrative job and is currently teaching at a university. Now his life has purpose and meaning. He had felt dead for so many years that he is determined to stay in this stage for a long time (perhaps the rest of his life). His marriage is in great shape and he is finally living a life he wants to live.

EXERCISE

Imagine that you are 18 again, but you know everything you now know. What would you do differently? What would be important to you? How would you spend your money? What would stop you from doing what you want?

Write this all out – use your imagination. Think about the classes you would take, the experiences you would have, and the dreams you would fulfill.

Now change your age from 18 to the age you are now. Begin to do all that you would have done at age 18 if you knew then what you know now. Turn the pain you've lived through into labor pains and give birth to your dreams.